Countries

India

by Christine Juarez

raintree
a Capstone company — publishers for children

Raintree is an imprint of Capstone Global Library Limited, a company incorporated in England and Wales having its registered office at 264 Banbury Road, Oxford, OX2 7DY – Registered company number: 6695582

www.raintree.co.uk
myorders@raintree.co.uk

Edited by Erika L. Shores
Designed by Bobbie Nuytten
Picture research by Tracy Cummins
Production by Laura Manthe

Printed in China
ISBN 978 1 4747 1980 3
20 19 18 17 16
10 9 8 7 6 5 4 3 2 1

British Library Cataloguing in Publication Data
A full catalogue record for this book is available from the British Library.

Photo Credits
Getty Images: The India Today Group, 5; iStockphotos: paresh3d, 22; Shutterstock: 29151112, 4, Aleksandar Todorovic, 1, Dmitry Kalinovsky, 11, Eduard Kyslynskyy, 9, GreenTree, 22, Im Perfect Lazybones, 17, JeremyRichards, 15, Joe Gough, 13, Jorg Hackemann, 19, Mazzzur, 21, Ohmega1982, back cover (globe), OPIS Zagreb, 7, Transia Design, cover, 1 (design element), turtix, cover,

We would like to thank Gail Saunders-Smith, Ph.D., for her invaluable help in the preparation of this book.

Every effort has been made to contact copyright holders of material reproduced in this book. Any omissions will be rectified in subsequent printings if notice is given to the publisher.

All the internet addresses (URLs) given in this book were valid at the time of going to press. However, due to the dynamic nature of the internet, some addresses may have changed, or sites may have changed or ceased to exist since publication. While the author and publisher regret any inconvenience this may cause readers, no responsibility for any such changes can be accepted by either the author or the publisher.

Note to Parents and Teachers

The Countries series supports learning related to people, places and culture. This book describes and illustrates India. The images support early readers in understanding the text. The repetition of words and phrases helps early readers learn new words. This book also introduces early readers to subject-specific vocabulary, which is defined in the Glossary section. Early readers may need assistance to read some words and to use the Contents, Glossary, Read more, Websites and Index sections of the book.

Contents

Where is India?

India is a country in southern Asia. It is almost three times the size of all the Scandinavian countries put together. New Delhi is India's capital city.

Landforms

India has many landforms. To the north are the River Ganges and the Himalayas. The Thar Desert is to the west. Mountains line the south-west and south-east coasts.

Animals

India has all kinds of animals.

Tigers and elephants roam India.

Cobras and other snakes live there.

Colourful birds, such as peacocks and parrots, make homes there, too.

Language and population

India is home to more than

1.2 billion people. Most people

live in small houses in rural villages.

People speak Hindi, English

or one of 14 other languages.

Food

Indians often eat spicy vegetable and meat curries. People sometimes scoop food with a flat bread called chapatti. Rice is often eaten with meals.

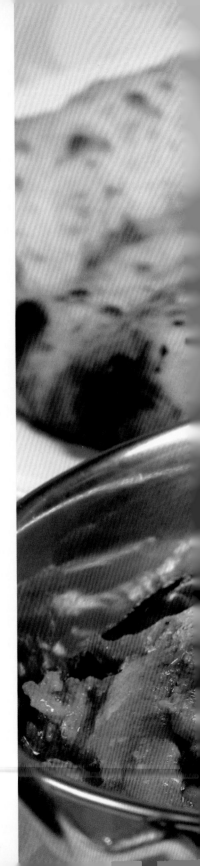

Celebrations

National holidays are important in India. Republic Day is on 26 January. Independence Day is on 15 August. People watch parades on these days.

Where people work

Most Indians work as farmers.
They grow rice and wheat. In cities,
Indians work in factories that
make clothing. Many people also
work in business or with computers.

Transportation

Many Indians ride motorbikes
or bicycles. They also travel
by rickshaw. A driver pedals
a bicycle attached to a cart
with one or two riders.

Famous sight

About 400 years ago, 20,000 workers and hundreds of elephants helped to build the Taj Mahal. It took 22 years to finish. It is India's most famous building.

Country facts

Name: Republic of India

Capital: New Dehli

Population: 1,220,800,359 (July 2013 estimate)

Size: 2,973,177 square kilometres (1,147,950 square miles)

Languages: Hindi, English and 14 other official languages

Main crops: rice, wheat, cotton, tea

India's flag

Money: rupee

Glossary

capital city in a country where the government is based

coast land next to an ocean or sea

cobra venomous snake

desert dry area with very little rain

factory place where a product is made

Himalayas mountain range in Asia; the world's tallest mountain, Mount Everest, is found in the Himalayas

landform natural feature of the land

language words used in a particular country or by a particular group of people

rural to do with the countryside

Read more

India: A Benjamin Blog and His Inquisitive Dog Guide (Country Guides), Anita Ganeri (Raintree, 2015)

The Indian Empire (Great Empires), Ellis Roxburgh (Wayland, 2015)

Websites

ngkids.co.uk/places/country-fact-file-india
Explore facts about India's history, goverment, culture and more.

www.timeforkids.com/destination/india
Learn all about India through photos and facts.

Index